The Spirit *Calls*

Joseph Raffa

The Spirit Calls

Author: Joseph Raffa

Editor: Teena Raffa-Mulligan

ISBN 978-0-9944990-1-1

eISBN 978-0-9872276-8-3

Author's note: The term 'mankind' is used throughout this discourse in reference to the human race collectively.

Published by Sea Song Publications

sea-song@bigpond.com

www.seasongpublications.com

.1.

SOON AFTER CHILDHOOD we settle into a humdrum acceptance of life. Growing up drives out the innocence, the freshness and the fascination with life. Of the time in the womb, the birth and early infancy it is rare to recall anything at all. After birth, much of the time is spent in sleep, just looking, listening and reaching out to touch. As surface awareness develops in experience and understanding, so does awareness of the self and the world about expands considerably.

Yet for years, through childhood and beyond we take self and surroundings for granted. We explore the outer, but we do not ponder the whys and wherefores. We do question our parents about who created us and the world and we take the answer "God did" with simple acceptance even though we do not understand the nature of this god or what parents mean by the word.

As youngsters on the move in this wide, wonderful world we do show a great deal of interest in our surrounds but this is more in the nature of exploring the outer display rather than a thoughtful investigation of life or of any deeper purpose in being here. Moving into adolescence we come into contact with the meaning of sex and so we learn the body is the product of a special union, conceived and nurtured in a mother's womb till the time of birth. This settles much of the uncertainty about our being here but it leaves unsolved the perplexing riddle of the continuous living process we are a part of. And then, there is the magnificent universe we read about, the multitude of stars we see at night, the comets that occasionally visit, the solar system — all this is grist for the inquiring imagination.

During our teen years we are more concerned with exploring new avenues of experience that are opening out and are far too busy savouring life rather than philosophising on the why and wherefore of anything. By this time, if we are avid readers we have come into contact with the scientific thought of the day, with the theory of evolution for life and the universe and also with religion, which challenges us with the idea of a creative power as the sole source of all things manifest.

Science strives to maintain an approach verifiable by experimentation and supported by logical reason to account for all presentable phenomena without recourse to a creative power. Such a power, intangible to the mind, unexplainable by the reasoning process, unverifiable by experiment would pose difficulties to the scientific mind. The evolutionary explanation and the big bang start to the universe sound impressive to the unenlightened. But the complex interrelationship of life with the environment, and the vastness of the universe that effortlessly maintains its balance, reflect something far more amazing and miraculous as a cause than mere mechanical interaction of chance changes or fortuitous development that somehow led to the sustained development of life and the universe we know today.

Religious thought too, has its difficulties. It cannot present a god wrapped in certitude nor can it convey with infallible evidence that God exists in a real sense rather than as a proffered belief or an intellectual concept until that blessed day when death calls and all is suddenly revealed. Somewhere along the way, as humans develop into adulthood, many begin to look seriously at the life they are a part of and begin to question the why and wherefore of it and to wonder if anything did make it happen as it has. And, being diverse in their backgrounds and outlooks, they gravitate in different directions in the search for answers. Thus were born the various philosophies and religious approaches. And science.

.2.

THOSE WHO CONSIDER themselves to be the most practical of people will have none of what they consider to be the airy fairy nonsense of a creative power and the attendant lore and thinking that goes with it. They turn to science and logical reason to supply the best answers. Eventually they expect the right answers will be found to all the puzzles presented by life. Their lives are built around an atheistic base of denial or an agnostic one that prefers to sit on the fence of neutrality until the issue is settled by new evidence.

Those who lean towards a religious approach to solve the difficulties posed by life and the universe are also in somewhat of a quandary. There are many of these, each with a distinctive offering to the masses. All have devoted adherents, eager to spread the word and show by example the quality of what they have. Or what in their eyes they believe they have.

There are people who walk the world today who are explorers in a very real sense. They want no part of chains that slavishly bind to the written word, to the authority of a book or a person, no matter how sacred the book or exalted the life of the person. The old ways do not attract, nor are they interested in difficult disciplines that deny natural human functions, relationships between the sexes and the raising of children. They are part of the social scene in which they live. They do not renounce society's ways and bury themselves in a quiet retreat for a lifetime of reflection and meditation until they find eternal bliss, peace or whatever else it may be called.

They begin the search for a higher meaning to life whilst immersed in the rapid flow of day to day living and preoccupied with the many chores that demand attention. Everyone has a beginning somewhere in time, and what gives a focus to this endeavour once it stirs into movement is a book or collection of writings by authors who write with inspiration and authority. Even should they disclaim the mantle of spiritual teachers and insist they are merely instruments of a higher purpose, yet still they speak and write in a style and with a conviction that commands attention and appeals to the searching mind. Once committed in this direction the interested seeker rearranges time to include study and redirects the attention, continually framing questions to further learning about the self and how it functions.

The background of the day's undertaking becomes, "What can I learn and what can I discover about myself that is helpful in this quest?" And not only from the surface and intellectual side is the approach fashioned but also deeper, from the inner side of human nature. The earnest seeker soon develops a strong conviction that much of what happens on the surface is projected from within and that the key to a higher understanding lies within; and is only partly dependent on the books that are read, the people who are listened to or even the reasons reflectively fashioned as clearways in a difficult journey.

This is not intended as an egotistical assertion that confines the seeker's approach solely to the self. Inasmuch that we approach learning and life through the mind and its depth of understanding, and that its conditioned background of influences and attitudes will be the active filter through which experiences are screened, judgements made and conclusions arrived at, it follows that the complex mind must be put in order first. If there is confusion here this will reflect in everything the mind thinks and does. Being clear is the essence of genuine understanding.

This is the main difficulty in self-learning — to see clearly as we proceed without being entangled too much in words and thinking, without being influenced by a complex background of experience, the books we've read, the information, attitudes and beliefs acquired. The mind is a storehouse of knowledge. Set a question and bingo, the mind will come up with an answer from its vast stock of information. This is not the same as being clear.

Clearview seeing is natural, direct and uncomplicated in its arisal. It sparkles in its penetration of human behaviour. Little activity is required by the thinking process to stir it into being, other than a setting of questions about some aspect of our nature and then leaving the matter be and allowing the inner side to deal with it in its own superior way. Interference by the mind must be avoided at all cost, consciously or unconsciously, and this is difficult. When the mind sets out on a course of questions, it instinctively wants to respond with the answers, and this means a response in reasonable terms with the conclusion presented to the surface attention.

The mind has a bent for manipulation in its search for learning about the self. Much of the background material isn't fresh but comes in the way of knowledge acquired from books. The main contenders to influence thinking are the accumulations of science and religion. Politics too, with its ideological concepts, is a heavyweight contender to gain and hold our allegiance. These influential strands, with others prevailing in the social mainstream, intermingle to form the basis of our daily living. What we come into contact with is sometimes vigorously presented but mostly it is a pervasive influence that affects us from an early age, through school where we learn the basics of human and social endeavour, and from the family, where established influences percolate inwards, beginning from birth.

As the self develops in standing, the educative input from family and society is overlaid with the individual thrust of the mind, which sees other considerations to be sought after and valued. This varies with the individual, but in the main, humans pass through an educative process by which society and family, either intentionally or by example, impose prevailing outlooks and attitudes on the young.

So by and large, we develop into the kind of humans that fit into, maintain and support the prevailing flow of the existing social units. And after years of involvement and being affected by this complex of intentions, attitudes and the like, it is very difficult to extricate the mind from the established mainstream of travel in the usual directions and redirect it on the new journey of self-discovery.

Our footprints are so muddied by constant travel in the sands of timeful experience that we soil every direction we move in. The mind takes an overload of contamination with it wherever it goes. Moments of sparkling clarity, unaffected by the conditioned background, do not arise. Yet this is what the mind needs to lighten its movement through life. Moments of spiritual impact that sweep away every vestige of the deep-rooted influences that living in timeful experience have imposed on the human expression. Years of conditioning are thrown off in an instant when the spiritual is abroad and active in the human entity.

The background influences are powerful and extensive. Various authorities are in control. Mostly, the mind is unaware of what is going on. Powerful authorities — religious, political, social, scientific, national, parental, educative — with a long history of application that reaches back in time. Its roots extend deep into the human psyche to stake a claim to various aspects of the individual expression so that humans are carved up into sections that belong to these authorities.

We are not integrated expressions — bold discoverers of our spiritual nature and the truth about ourselves. We are directed in much of what we think, say and do by the prevailing trends that dominate the social climate of the day. And these in turn are the products of a past that have grown from small beginnings, been nurtured along the way by extension, accumulation and expanding power via the imposition of authority until they have become the present day establishments. Individuals are swept along in the momentum generated by these authorities like so much debris caught up in a powerful tidal motion.

From the time our eyes first open to the fascinating world around us, the moulding process begins. Only lightly at first, for we are too sleepy to be of much use to those who are waiting to shape us, but as we more vigorously awaken, so the established agencies move to absorb us into the prevailing social mainstream. Enquiry is allowed in a society as long as it is not construed to be a threat to the status quo. Support is what the establishment wants, not a revolutionary approach that may undermine or terminate its authority.

Where a trend has been in existence for centuries and the supportive roots are deep and the ramifications wide, the pressures on individuals to conform are considerable. There is much to lose, particularly in some countries, if the establishment is openly confronted. Jail without trial, loss of secure jobs and property, home confinement for long periods without recourse to justice or contact with the media, banishment abroad, separation from families, torture or even death. These have been some of the ways in which established authority protects its position.

In the societies where such excesses have been put aside there is still a deep-rooted expectation that insists on individual support. No rocking the social boat, no challenging the foundations of the mainstream of established attitudes. Be prepared to face a critical backlash if you do. The authorities in a society have dedicated devotees who vigorously support, defend and work to expand the organisations and authority in control. This supportive activity will continue as long as it brings worthwhile benefits as a consequence. Individuals intend to reap a harvest of benefits through what they do and this intention determines the extent and persistence of the involvement and the depth of support for the authority in control.

.3.

OCIAL ENSLAVEMENT IS difficult to counter. People grow gradually into this kind of conditioning. Language, social customs, national outlooks, religious and political arrangements, all these and more set fertile seeds in susceptible minds. An extensive input moulds the individual mind into the prevailing social framework. Within the national boundaries the predominant trends and influences determine much of the nature of individual development. New arrivals from abroad hold to their own background for as long as they can but eventually they too are influenced to the degree that they yield and adopt the new ways.

The social atmosphere pulses with the intention to extend its influence deep into each and every human component born into or accepted within its confines. This purpose is constantly nurtured and no effort is spared to cultivate the human material in every way. This is not only by deliberate intention. There is a pervading subconscious influence established deep within the controlling centres set up to maintain the social status quo.

The prevailing social directives, once established, have a bent for perpetuating the intention to foster, preserve, strengthen and enlarge the social units under control. The overall purpose (tenaciously held to), is to maintain the constancy and the characteristics of the national and state systems. This is, in a sense, a seductive system of mind control all the more effective because it is tacitly accepted by those who come under the control of the social influence.

It is rare for people to generate resistance to every aspect of the social system they are born into or adopt. They may resent some parts of it and set out to change them through whatever means are available. By and large, the social arrangements afford such security and protection that people would be loath to entirely dismantle them without a concrete replacement they could wholeheartedly support. Otherwise, it would be like stripping away everything they have relied on, leaving themselves naked, exposed and vulnerable.

We fail to see how deeply we are shaped into national and social moulds that make us slaves to systems of divisive intent, that separate us into self-seeking groups primarily bent on our own salvation and economic advantage. While narrow separatist interests are abroad and active there is little scope for international unity and purpose to step in and effectively deal with global matters. Even with alliances that draw diverse people together for self protection or economic improvement, basic differences persist and come to the surface when difficulties arise. These often determine the outcome of actions pursued, which are then settled on the basis of national interests rather than on the merits of the situations that exist.

In the early stages of the journey into social arrangements, there was probably little organised contamination of consequence at the beginning. But the possibility existed and by the time humans had spent many years in the social conditioning chamber, they hardened into fully supportive members of the society they were born into. This then became their measuring rod for living, the basic background that determined outlooks and attitudes towards themselves and outsiders. By this social accumulation they judge not only the measure of their appreciation of life but also the worth of what they are, of what they have and also the value of societies in comparison with their own.

Needless to say, they are generally predisposed towards their own system — its traditions, lifestyles, customs, cultural expressions and suchlike. Having grown up with these since birth, there is a familiar ring to what goes on, a comfortable feel to surroundings, to people and places and the ways they have grown up with. Nor would people question these arrangements unless driven by a deep discontent to do so.

.4.

W ITH POWERFUL INFLUENCES active, inwardly and outwardly controlling and shaping the mind into supporting the prevailing social arrangements, what scope is there for individuals to disentangle themselves from the complex stranglehold of influences and emerge creatively fresh and inwardly free of this social suffocation? First of all, there must be a declared intention. If the situation as it exists is wholeheartedly accepted, no inward response will stir to remedy the situation. There must be an acknowledgement, a determination to unravel the content of the social conditioning operating in the individual.

The influences are only understood when they are relayed onto a conscious screen for introspection and impartial assessment. Otherwise the mind is not in a position to deal with, understand and evaluate the way they operate in the individual psyche. Accepting and supporting this complex input from an early age, without question, allows an unhindered growth of the social input and social control of the human expression. While the social conditioning is in control, freedom is only a word and not a fact of life. The choices that are made are in some way determined by this overriding background. It has been the dominant influx in our lives from birth. We are not warned about its effects nor encouraged to investigate the consequences impartially with unrestricted awareness. Not looking inwardly, we do not know what is going on in our minds.

Rather, we are educated and encouraged to accept the social ways that surround us. And the education has one main purpose — to explain the social extent, to emphasise its importance, to preserve its operation and to fit the individual into the social organisation. The emphasis is on the value of social aims, characteristics and organisations, the security it provides, the range of options on offer for variety and interesting living.

The mood of the social movement operates to draw into its fold all the people who are considered by law, tradition, by national extent as belonging to the social organisation that imposes its authority over a land area and its resident people.

The purpose of this writing is, in effect, an invitation to all people, regardless of background, to challenge this complex of influences that is shaping behaviour, thinking and actions. Not only to challenge it with reasonable endeavour but with action from the highest level of all — the spiritual. To wage the battle for control of the human expression solely on reasonable forays, on logical introspection is to wage a war that never ends. Action remains securely anchored on the level where words and thoughts are the supreme weapons of involvement. Reducing social influences to words and their meanings doesn't take the mind to the heart of the matter. Rational thinking initiated by a socially controlled self cannot expose the inner nature of the influences that impact on and shape the mind.

It requires a challenge from a deeper level of our being. Action is needed from the unconscious level, from that subtle extent where influences are grafted into the human psyche and control points are set up to further feed and strengthen the accepted input. Once established, social influences reign with dictatorial authority, directing thoughts, behaviour and speech, the process being enacted in such a subtle manner and with individual compliance that those controlled are unaware of the nature of the growth that has attached itself to the human expression. When the social input is deeply established the individual becomes an outlet for and a continuation of the surrounding social influences.

Language, standpoint, outlook on life, on other people and cultures, and lifestyle patterns are very much a product of the social background. To a large extent this determines behaviour, viewpoints, judgements and much of the direction of the individual travel along the highway of life. The totality of the social input cannot be disregarded. Society supplies the working tools for day to day living. People cannot revert to a blankness of not knowing and still function in a purposeful way. Some part of this social background, of necessity, we will keep as we live out our day to day experiences. But we can stir ourselves out of complete acceptance and move to understand this complex involvement between individuals and the tide of influences and ideas that pours in to establish bases of control from within.

Establishment and acceptance are the first steps to social consolidation once the inner extent of the self has been breached by steady and familiar application. The mind is avid for experience and a supportive framework to sustain and guide its progress down the highway of life. It absorbs information, attitudes and influences that prevail in its surroundings. Providing these are agreeable and not disturbing in any way, the boom gates of the mind are lowered and this input is allowed entry with its mass of social characteristics.

The grafting process that follows is subtle and effortless. So much so that inevitably the self will take on much of the surrounding influences in the way of mannerisms, speech, dress, social behaviour and thinking. The mind assumes the mask of its surroundings. Through this acquisition it sees, thinks, chooses, judges, and while this persists it can only know what this mask permits it to know. The acquired background (the mask) acts as a clearing house for all the information and experiences the mind comes into contact with. Everything is evaluated in relationship to the base, sorted out, allowed entry if the ruling is affirmative, discarded if otherwise. In this way, the inner establishment's control is strengthened and not diminished.

Accepting the base and acting from it is the most complex and devious of expressions to roam the plains of timeful experience — the personal "I", the "Me", the troublemaker of time. The stubborn core that manifests as desire, demand, choice, and insists on self-return, achievement, enhancement and satisfaction through what it does. The background shapes the self and in turn the self presides over the background, tending it like a gardener caring for the garden. The outer forging the inner background, the inner responding to strengthen and protect the acquired base. The process continues until people completely succumb to social control or until they rise with revolutionary fervour, take up the razor sharp axe of an understanding not manipulated by the background and begin to cut away the tangled growth of imposed attitudes. By the light of this new understanding they will see the background has prevented a clear approach to living, sullied the pristine awareness of the living process and subverted the role of the individual in the movement of life.

The dawning of this new understanding is a difficult art indeed.

It is not a product of past experience nor forged from accumulated knowledge, no matter how worthy the source. Neither is it the result of the skilful use of reason, that interplay of words and thoughts expressing logical effect and disarming postures of infallible edicts. Rather, it is a completely new arisal born of a strange union. Not of disparate natures, but of essentially similar and indistinguishable levels of being.

One, the fundamental nature of the human expression; the other, the underlying Universal Nature. This intermingling signals the beginning of the end of the isolated functioning of the individual entity and its past total reliance on a socially acquired base of distinguishing characteristics. An end in the sense that the base is relegated from its former authoritarian control of the human expression and gradually emasculated by the impact of revelatory insights that follow the advent of this unifying moment in the individual life.

Those aspects of our background that do not hinder the harmonious expression of our spiritual nature continue to operate. These are necessary in day to day living. But the devious intentions of the self to establish itself in its social surrounds — in a base of adopted ideas and attitudes that limit the human expression — are relentlessly exposed and dealt with by an unyielding understanding that pursues the self through every facet of its endeavour to continue along a pathway of its own determination. Form and reform its approach as it will, it cannot escape what is set into motion by the arisal of the Universal Nature in its life.

.5.

THE BATTLE TO preserve the self along the lines of its own choosing is a long and hard fought one. Every protection it can devise is brought to the forefront in a wearing war of attrition that time and again batters the mind into stalemate or submission as it sees, by the insights released, the folly and futility of its efforts to bring about worthwhile improvements and the inadequacy of its shallow understanding to deal with the challenges of life.

Always the incurable optimist, the self rises again and again to challenge the sovereignty of this new presence in its life. It cannot accept that its initiative and determinations are of little consequence in the matter of clear view living, not even in that area it considers its very own private domain. So it rallies time and time again after some frank and hard-hitting disclosures to blithely return in much the same directions that appeared to yield desirable support in its daily journey through the garden of timeful experience.

But humans belong firstly to Universal Life and secondly to the world of time and experience. No matter how long the sojourn in the latter, and in spite of the insistence to carve out a durable niche according to personal specifications, it is to this life force all must inevitably return. We can hold to our traditions with tenacity; to our social constitutions and institutions with limpet-like persistence; to the extensive and complex background of knowledge, experience and attitudes we rely on with such unshakeable faith. All this and the surface self we will hold to, but, in spite of the stubborn resistance that all this individual activity raises to this calling from the "Strangeness" side of our being, back we will surely make our way when we cannot stand the pain of this spiritual separation any longer.

Humans must have a home they can acknowledge as the only true home. We have built our establishments in time and labelled these home. On these, we've lavished care and protection and poured physical and mental energy into their protection, expansion and preservation. Our faces are turned to the god of material and mental security and our backs to our spiritual homeland. We deny its existence by every utterance and by our daily actions. We no longer walk tall, sublime in our spiritual nature, but rather are parodies of what the human expression should be. Our thoughts darken the skies of everyday living and human behaviour shatters what should be a peaceful and happy life.

Social living has become a tangle of contradictions, a nightmare of concerns and confusion. Day by day, the strain of the separation from the spiritual strangeness supplies varying evidence of the heartbreak, the hardships and disturbing behaviour that follows as a consequence of this estrangement. In the protection of the national fold we go to sleep and ignore the urgent need to return to our creative homeland.

We prefer to occupy ourselves with the cultivation of that side of living that is exclusively concerned with the many demands of surface living. Such is the nature of the problems that arise, of needs, desires and intentions, that the mind's attention flows outward to meet this extent, this focus of human endeavours in living. It fills to saturation with the affairs of time, soaked brimful, dealing with one thing after another.

Constantly tuned to an outward focus, it is difficult for the mind to reverse the flow and redirect the attention inwards with one underlying purpose — the discovery of its relationship with the Universal Strangeness. Indeed, should this be its intention, such is the state of conditioning from the acquired background that it complicates the journey in diverse ways, raising no end of difficulties in its immature attempts to lay claim to the universal nature. This cannot be avoided in the beginning. With the mind cluttered inwardly with the results of misdirected thinking, imbued with a strong sense of individual separation, these raise expectations that have no valid basis in the search for that which is Universal — in which separation does not exist.

Humans have gone the present ways not by accident but rather by choice, inclination and reasonable design. Whatever challenges have come their way they have responded according to the level of understanding and usually without recourse to a divine directive. Humans are responsible for whatever difficulties have followed, apart from those inflicted by nature over which there is as yet no control.

The close contact they once enjoyed with the natural world and with the divine nature has been replaced with an expanding intellectual expression centred on a self that sees little need for a divine directive in its life. This intellectualism covers every aspect of the living process with reasonably determined classifications and descriptions. An avalanche of words, thoughts, reasons pours relentlessly out of the mind. Explanations and descriptions intervene between the mind and everything that takes place, inwardly and outwardly.

This overlay, this reasonable assemblage, distilled from the ordinary level of understanding, backed by a swollen sense of self-importance, has become a formidable barrier, denying humans a fresh, new vision and an intimate contact with the Sparkle of Life. So much so that verbal explanations and reasonable presentations have become more important than direct discovery, than immediate contact with the creative arisal of the universal interplay that surrounds us.

The expanding expression of the intellectual capacity dominates with thought-filled intent and presides with reasonable authority over the human expression. It maintains and extends its position through intense and extensive use, aided and abetted by the customary and unquestioned acceptance by humans that it should be the sole overlord in human affairs. Consequently, humans lose the intimate contact with life that is active in the very young and supplant this with the sterile explanations and complex procession of an overloaded intellectual activity.

Now we do not live attention wrapped in the present but project complicated patterns as bridges to travel along in our endeavours to preserve the narrow interest and programs of the self in action. The actor is the self, the theatre is the extension of the self and the scenario is devised by the self. Only when the challenges of life arise to disturb this movement by the mind towards self-establishment in every direction is the self forced to check its usual travel and re-examine its values and attitudes towards itself, others and its surrounds.

And this is often just for the time it takes to settle back into the accustomed channels the self is familiar with, for the furrows of social intercourse are deep and well defined. The individual is not inclined to leave the safety of timeworn travel in the usual directions, neither by self-determination nor by coercion from outer circumstances.

It takes a powerful impetus from within to turn us from our well-worn social path to travel the timeless way to a new dimension of existence. The impulse to move on a spiritual quest may arise in response to outer difficulties that appear insoluble, to the impact of disturbing and continuous pain, to the failure of our deepest expectations when the returns for our efforts do not match urgent desires, or it may be due to a prolonged discontent that refuses to be dissolved whatever we do.

It matters little what the spur is. What is important is that we declare our intentions, mean what we say, set the mind in motion and persist in holding this quest for spiritual discovery in the forefront of attention. A weak-willed intention will not take people very far in this journey. A persistent desire, driven by the urgency to discover, is paramount. The distractions in the outside world are many and varied and will test human resolve to the utmost, but the truly dedicated will not be swayed by the offerings on display in the garden of timeful experience, no matter how appealing and desirable.

Not that the travel is, in any way, a steady line of progress. Humans are much too fickle for that and likely to oscillate between the extremes of inspired application and the despair of unrealised dreams. There are highs and lows, and to the seeker who breaks through the timeful barriers that chain the mind rigidly to its earthly surrounds, to the fleshly body; who circumvent the damaging effects of living in self-centred isolation and viewing life from the confines of the senses, the delight when discovery makes its initial impact is something to be experienced in the exhilaration and the uplifting release that follows.

.6.

THE NARROW CONFINES of the self are shattered by the expansiveness of the Universal Strangeness — this spiritual nature that yields a harvest of blessings at the moment of discovery. Here, we are dealing with the inexplicable, with the meeting between what many call God and its human offspring. And the meeting is on God's hallowed ground. In a swift moment we are transported away from the projection of the self we are familiar with into a wonderland of being. Completeness rules here, a oneness beyond our ken, and its coming lights up the human expression with an understanding that the world of timeful experience cannot supply, nor the endeavours of the mind ever match.

Now humans begin to move with the Universal Tide of Life in harmony with its rhythm. A new learning has begun and the reasoning process now has a basis for action that is clear and revelatory. An energetic movement is abroad, stirring the human expression into peaceful and revolutionary change. A change born of discovery, forged by a fresh understanding, independent of human will or intention. And what a profound effect on the human psyche as the winds of change gather force from the spiritual beyond and blow with increasing frequency over the human land.

All manner of upheavals, mental and emotional erupt into the conscious light of daily living. The kaleidoscope of moods swings through joyous ecstasy, exhilarating releases, deep contentment to dark despair and despondency, even tears depending on the nature of the revelations that flow into conscious awareness. But the awakening from a former, deadening inner sleep cannot be denied.

The mind is astir and on the move, refreshed and recharged from an amazing spiritual source — the magical essence of life. Thinking as the leading directive in human affairs is brushed aside momentarily as the universal sensitivity comes to the forefront. No fanfare of trumpets greets its arrival. No banners proclaim its presence. Unheralded, unsung, no waiting throngs to cheer and wave. Just suddenly it is there, everywhere. God and the human expression, bonded together in a loving unity, without distinction or difference.

The self that roamed the highways and byways of time, surged into the seas of experience, drifted through desire and experienced the delights and pain of sensation, soared with hope like a high flying eagle and plummeted into the depths of despair has been washed clean of stain, its immediate capacity for illusion dissolved in one swift moment of discovery. Something vital and indelibly clear has taken place. A shift from the old level of the mind and its dependency on words, ideas, experience, reason. What is discovered is beyond this, beyond the grasp of the mind. Space and time have been circumvented and the enchanting world of instant awareness has taken over. Here, the Universal Strangeness holds timeless sway.

That "which is", which alone is enduringly real, has come into the human expression. It becomes established as the primary directive, replacing the former authority of reason and the outer social authorities that controlled humans for various purposes, encouraging the support of systems based on separation and a denial of the unitary nature of humankind.

The Universal is our natural home. Inevitably, sometime, when we weary of time-ridden journeying, we shall return. There is nowhere else to go but back to the spiritual homeland from where we first arose to journey forth into timeful experience. Here, restless feet will come to rest in an undisturbed Universal repose. The self will be silenced by its immensity and wonder: reason will be humbled by its ungraspable mystery; the mind will be stripped of its mental possession and given in return the very essence of its own nature. And nothing will be left the self in the way of achievement, nothing in the way of mental accumulations. All that exists as an enduring certainty, as a constant reality, is the mysterious essence, the fundamental nature of the Universal Strangeness.

Only this is never ending, has true immortality, and so we too, not as a knowing and individual self but as this nature which we share, are also never ending. In terms of the mind's understanding, by logical reason, there is little that can be comprehended about this deeper existence. Yet it is the gateway to peace and harmony, to an expanded new learning that comes from a divine source and has immeasurable value for us. And as such its directives and the insights released are of crystal clarity, surging at times with illuminating freshness through the darkness of the mind.

Mere mortals are we on the surface side. Our individuality, no matter how long its measure in years, is just a brief page in the story of human life. But on the highest level of all we have a nature untouched by the ravages of time. Here, we are corrosion free. The sparkle of springtime surges within. Yet how often our face is turned towards the security of time, towards our social side. We take the image in the mirror to be our real face and ignore our unknown one.

Will humans ever hunger with passionate fervour for the Universal Nature of which they are part? How much longer will they remain anchored in time, reaching for the offerings that glow with the colours of desire and neglect their inner development? The mind is mesmerised by its surrounds, by the social interplay going on. Its journey is a one-way direction — outward bound.

Like a boat sailing down the river of time into fresh vistas of absorbing experiences. Impressed by this colourful interplay, by the colour and form, by the sounds and the feels, by the intimate connection with the body, the underlying reality of our spiritual nature goes unnoticed. The mind is far too busy with the separate parts of appearance to reach out for the whole. The parts are valued — the total ignored.

What can be held in the hands, what can be touched, seen, felt and heard is given value.

Because the whole (the Universal) cannot be held, cannot be seen nor apprehended through the senses or the reasoning process, for the mind it has no worthwhile value in comparison, nor is it considered important in human living. So the mind goes to sleep in time and consequently suffers. Estranged from its source it has no protection from illusion and misunderstanding, from the arisal of evil and sinister movements. The deeper understanding and insights are not active to prevent this from happening. Humans become the unwitting tools for their own destruction, for disruption to flow into surface living, and inwardly they wither from the lack of spiritual nourishment.

The body is nourished in time. The mind and the emotional side are fed with a variety of stimulating and entertaining experiences, but somehow we cannot feed on the most nourishing food of all — spiritual sustenance from the fountainhead of life. This only comes from contact with the universal source, from the discovery of and union with the source. In this there is renewal, freshness and regeneration. A cleansing process washes away the contamination of living in time. The cataracts that obscure human vision are expertly removed by a master surgeon using the instruments of love, wisdom and a super understanding. Humans emerge as new people from these delightful moments of universal discovery.

The tide of the mind, the shadows it cast over human living are rolled back, dissolved by the advent of an enhanced awareness. The inner side of the human expression, formerly inaccessible to observation and overlaid with the dust of years of accumulation from the surface side, opens out and the Sunshine of Life floods in. Descriptions, no matter how inspired, cannot convey the new sensitivity that awakens following the coming of the Divine Strangeness. It is something humans have to be a part of, have to discover for themselves. Those who hunger deeply, who are carried forward on a wave of discontent with ordinary living, have a chance of eventually breaking through. Their hearts are in the search, longing for something that is missing from their lives.

And even though the mind raises obstacle after obstacle that bars access to this timeless nature, there are moments when the activity of the mind is exhausted, when human effort is exhausted and the self is put aside. In these moments of self-absence, when silence takes over, the opportunity is there for discovery to happen, for the human expression to enter a state of enlightenment. The illusions that formerly held sway and distorted the mind's vision are swiftly dispelled. The mind sees clearly into its nature, into its motives for living, without prejudice or self-distortion. It is liberating to see in such a manner.

Such moments wash away the stultifying effects of weary months or years of human effort based on the mind's limited level of understanding. The chains that link the mind to a surface standing and the anchors that hold us in time are tenacious indeed. They cannot be broken by self-effort or intention. Everything the self does strengthens the chains and intensifies the links with a background in which the self is the centre of action. In constant motion in this way, it cannot shift from the level of expression it is accustomed to. This activity, generated by the self, the inner and outer aspects, must naturally cease for the realisation of the Universal to take place. The storm of the self must subside if the calmness of the Universal is to be. As the known fades, the unknown comes out into the open and reveals its nature — its existence as a reality in its own right.

It's so natural when it happens. Nothing premeditated about it, no prior preparation. No contribution by the self helps in this harvest of discovery. The issue of what we are and what we come from is immediately settled. So too, is the question of whether God exists. This new knowledge is based on discovery, on the illumination that follows discovery. It is based on an infallible source.

Personal illumination is what inspires those touched by the Universal Strangeness. This casts the light that cleans out the contamination that would otherwise overwhelm the freshness of the human approach to living. It is this fallout from time, accepted and adapted by self-inclination that prevents humans functioning from the highest level of being. A fusion of social and personal attitudes, demands and desires takes over to direct the human expression into channels determined by the predominant background trends. This may be a matter of choice, of habits forged by social customs or directed by strong desires. This becomes the basis for most of our actions. While this functions it gives an emphasis to our individuality, to the sense of separateness and purpose to the self as a centre of distinction. As long as the self continues in this manner, it remains centre stage, at the forefront of the human expression. Any other side to human nature hasn't a chance of making a showing, regardless of the intention to investigate.

.7.

FIRMLY ANCHORED IN the attitudes that the self is separate from its surrounds and the body is exclusively itself, should it move to discover any other dimensions of existence it still expects to be there as a distinctive observer. The self has the intention to persist and maintain its cohesion and base in whatever field it moves in. It casts exploring tentacles in many directions through reason and imagination. Behind its endeavours is the desire to strengthen its movement, expand its base and be in control of its deliberations and travels. It's a way of being self-assertive and maintaining its continuity with expanding influence.

To proceed in the directions of its choices, to establish itself in its findings — to dwell in the flow of experiences and gain enhancement thereby and build a haven of comfort and security in time — all this is something of considerable importance to the self. Its energy therefore and its purpose develops a supportive base to protect and permit the progression of the self and its extensions. With the advent of self-existence, we have a situation whereby the Oneness of the universal nature is covered by a freewheeling expression that draws unto itself the mind's flow of attention. The focus of awareness is on the body, the surrounding environment, the sensations that arise, the flow of thinking and the variable emotional response. This is the self's known existence and it effectively blocks out any cognizance of the Divine Nature as a reality in its own right.

Through a legacy of written lore left to the human races by spiritual explorers in the past, there lingers the belief in the existence of a universal nature. Encouragement in the present has been added by those who claim union with this nature. Communication is by words and reason. The difficulty is that even when this is truthfully stated from inspired sources, this cannot by itself initiate others as a matter of course. It is, however, how the initial approach begins.

In as much that the thinking process and communication are reflections of the self, are brought into being and maintained by the self, their expression continues its movement on familiar levels and keeps it confined within its own activity. This cannot be otherwise even if the intention of the self is the discovery of its relationship with the Universal Nature. To move along avenues determined by the self is to remain on the road of self-projection. How then, could this lead to the nature of "that" which is beyond the self? Effort gives the self something to be absorbed in, a highway to move along that, in its own eyes, will eventually lead it away from the personal it knows to the Universal, which is the unknown.

This constant projection of the self is a persistent theme that needs to be understood, otherwise it can lead into unproductive avenues and dead ends and necessitate a re-evaluation of its purposes. This means reflection — an arduous undertaking — not something that comes easy to the self which prefers an easy road to travel. It would rather avoid the hard work of assessment and readjustment that often follows the arisal of insights into its nature, uncertain as to where this is leading it. The customary ways of living and thinking are so much easier. Any difficulties that come its way at least occur on a level it is familiar with and the approach it settles on is one that agrees with its sensibility on the matter.

It is unusual for the self to shift from the accepted social and individual grooves forged over years of acceptance and experience. These, if not always comfortable, are yet, to human understanding, preferable to moving in a new, untried direction, the relative importance of which is unverifiable beforehand and one that has to be taken on trust. It takes some kind of inner or outer pressure to urge the self away from its downhill travel in time — a preoccupation that is the focus of the mind's attention. This movement is awash with experience and here, the self is at home.

But pressures do arise — pain, loss, a sudden desire to know the truth about life, discontent with what we are and do and perhaps even a marked disinclination to accept the customary social values in their entirety. The initial impetus lodges in the mind and cannot be ignored. This sparks the mind into action, on the intellectual level firstly. This is the gateway through which the self enters on a new adventure. Then progressively inwards — into levels below the surface — stirring feelings, until the total content of the human expression awakens as to its true nature.

Most of the journey is revelatory in nature. After the initial intellectual grounding, such is the new learning that without assistance from a higher source the mind cannot fruitfully proceed due to its inability, through its own efforts, to shift from the field it knows to what lies beyond this. This help comes from a divine source. Although this journey begins by individual intention and application in the directions that are considered useful in the quest, it comes to fruition by divine intervention and assistance. The self does the hard work of bruising itself, the wear and tear that gets it nowhere special, all the twisting, turning and over-reaching it is capable of; but the arisal of a deeper understanding and the release that follows are born of a sharing by the Universal of its nature with the human entity.

Self-effort is useful to a point. This forms the backdrop of a collective experience pushing towards an expectant goal. The motives involved and the lack of effectiveness to bring about change are clearly exposed when discovery happens and insights are released. In this way the mind learns about its capacity for illusion, of how it creates and sustains effort in the hope of eventual spiritual reward. As it continues to change and redirect its movements, discarding old standpoints, reassessing and reforming its approach, so it learns the depth and variety of its capacity to extend and establish itself in the search. By intention, the mind keeps itself in the limelight, in the forefront of its actions.

The deeper the understanding of this movement, the more it loses its intensity and its

THE SPIRIT CALLS · 55

influence on those deeper levels that are beyond surface introspection. There are mental power points — strong centres of influence below the surface that trigger reactions and initiate momentum in variable directions according to the circumstances that arise or the choices made. This is translated into mental, emotional and physical action. It is important that what flows from these control points is for the good of mankind and not just in service of the personal self and its limited selfish interests.

Today, individual freedom is extolled as the highest virtue, particularly the freedom to choose political and social structures. A desirable lifestyle too, is given a great deal of emphasis. These, along with religious freedom, are considered most important. Very little consideration is given to another kind of freedom — the freedom to investigate the human content and social relationships, to discover the truth about the human expression and its relationship to the Universal.

Being a composite of physical, mental, emotional and spiritual, it follows if there is underdevelopment in any of these the approach to life will be disjointed and lack harmony. The results of any imbalance will show in the behaviour and thinking expressed and be reflected in the societies we create to regulate our lives. There is a great deal of emphasis on the outer aspects of human relationships and these are dealt with in the usual reasonable way. They are approached from a surface level of understanding and not from an understanding released from an integrated level of being.

The customary level conditions the approach and determines the conclusions. It is the main basis for action and while it functions, versatile and capable as it is to a marked degree, it is still locked into the weakness and limitations inherent in this particular approach. The imbalance that affects human understanding is clearly reflected in its societies. Side by side with technological advances, with progressive living and economic riches, there is difficulty in keeping pace with changing technology, there is starvation and poverty, disorder, corruption, pollution of the planet and violence.

The mind can understand many things, complex things, yet it seems it cannot understand itself, what its fundamental nature is — its role in the social organisation or how to relate without friction arising in its relationships. Above all, no common purpose comes to the fore to link humans together worldwide. Surface differences, racial, national or otherwise keep people separated into groups that are often antagonistic to others who are different in outlook and social organisation. Clearly, there is a lack of spiritual awareness in the attitudes reflected and the disturbing troubles that arise to plague humanity.

Spiritual awareness is the integrating factor that brings humans together in common purpose. Harmony and togetherness prevail, rather than discord and antagonisms. When the spiritual is active, the individual falls within its influence. The cast iron grip of the intellect is broken. Awareness breaks free from its surface bonds, from the limits of thought, experience and known phenomena and reverts naturally to universal awareness. In this state the self is absent. No self — no distinction. No problems, no difficulties.

This is true liberation — to be liberated from the self, from the projections of the mind, from the tyranny of time, from the influences of the known. To be momentarily adrift in a timeless, selfless state — this is the essence of living. From this meeting the human expression distils the finest that life has to offer. Time is only a pleasant mirage that shimmers on the horizon of the mind — the lure that draws us away from the wonder of what we are in essence.

The return to the Universal Strangeness fulfils life's purpose for the human race. We've wandered far in our surface meanderings, tried many things and lost ourselves in a maze of byways that led nowhere of enduring value. We've nourished the body, fed the mind and the emotions with stimulating experiences that satisfied for a time. But we have no solid grounding, no enduring foundations to build on. We've relied on the social constructs of the mind, organised ourselves to preserve the self and its extensions.

Social and material security has been fashioned to make our sojourn in time as comfortable as can be. But because our spiritual heritage has been denied, we have fallen foul of a host of troubles and these continue to intensify in spite of the methods devised to deal with them. It is no accident that we are confronted with difficulties. Nor is the blame due to a lack of experience. We will never be in a situation where we will have pre-experience of tomorrow's problems, tomorrow's difficulties. We are being brought face to face with our own creations. What we are capable of is projected outwardly and comes back to haunt us until such time as we understand how we are responsible.

And it will not end until we set out to discover the deeper resources that creative nature has blessed us with. Resources that are denied by the way we live, think, behave and organise ourselves. Intellectually, we know the story. Through the advent of spiritually inspired people on this planet we have been given evidence of the nature of these inner resources and the remarkable improvement that follows in human relationships when the spiritual is realised.

The self does not easily let go the directions it has chosen to travel in. And it is reluctant to devote itself in a search that from a surface viewpoint seemingly offers little of useful value. It well knows the value of money, of possessions, of a prominent standing in the community, of the security to be gained through organisation. This kind of value it can confidently assess. But the other kind, which is referred to as spiritual, in the beginning has little or nothing in the way of evidence to evaluate and therefore there is not the attraction in comparison to what a materialistic society has to offer.

Should it consider a religious approach, these are variable in what they offer. There is also disagreement over the meaning of the word and often, little in the behaviour and speech of those who follow a chosen creed to inspire the self to leave its social niche and set off on a journey of self-discovery. One in which the main aim is to realise the strange sensitivity that lies beyond the vale of space and time.

So it settles for the usual social travel, carries on somehow, gets jolted by trouble now and then and, from time to time, in the hope of social improvement, changes the politicians in charge of the nation.

Yet if the impetus for change doesn't begin with the individual, where is it to come from? Even those who await a Messiah, from whatever direction, will have to act differently if change is to sweep over this world. Otherwise, inspired sources will be ignored and things will continue much as they are. It is the human material that needs transforming. That means you and me.

The self, blind to its own contribution, is fond of thinking that it is A-OK and that others are more responsible for the troubles that abound. But in some way it adds a share to the troubles close by, and through the interlocking power of organisation it is responsible for the structure of authority and the way it operates through the social structure. Ultimately, the leaders can only do what the people permit them to do. If they are enlightened people, securely established in their spiritual nature, they will project enlightened leadership, spiritually awake and devoid of narrow self-centred viewpoints that focus on state, party or just national interests.

Likewise, if people are not spiritually active and deeply versed in self-understanding, they will project a different kind of leadership and a variety of difficulties that, in spite of experts educated and trained to deal with these situations, will compound with passing time and threaten the stability of the societies they value.

.8.

D O PEOPLE REALLY want profound change, or just piddling change? Are they prepared to make the effort — to devote themselves to a deeper self-understanding, to the discovery of that side of human nature that the word spiritual truly relates to? Or would they rather forge a comfortable niche in the social field where they could fashion their lifestyles with a minimum of disturbance and enjoy themselves as best they can while others take care of the troublesome issues in life?

Humans are like water running downhill. We tend to take the line of least resistance. Not for us the battle of surging uphill, against the established status quo. Rather, to move with the social flow of the times is the inclination, provided that what we are moving with doesn't bother us too much nor interfere with the enjoyment of life.

In any society, the basic components are the people. They are the building blocks out of which society is fashioned. The quality of the human material is very important, for out of the individual contribution, the social character for good or otherwise is effectively forged. Even when leaders wield immense power, such power comes from a compliant people. Whether it is offered voluntarily or reluctantly doesn't matter much. The support is there and this makes the operating structure of authority effective.

Before a fundamental change can take place throughout society, it must be realised firstly in the human components in that society. When this is actual in the individual, ongoing rather than a dream or an intention, the ground is set for a new social approach that will affect all the strata of the social organisation. And this approach will be energetic and flexible, taking care of every contingency that arises.

Such people are not stereotypes, nor the product of any present system. The schools of the day will not produce such people. They are forged from a different mould, and although they attend the school of life, the teacher is not of this world but of another dimension of existence than the one we know.

Using the classroom of the mind and the lessons of experience, with the blackboard of discovery to demonstrate the truth about human nature and behaviour, this unknown teacher will lead humans into enlightened living and a gentler expression of their nature. A wider awareness will spread its wings — break free from the hold of self-centred activity and soar in the timeless skies of Universal Being.

These are not fanciful words, not empty rhetoric but an actuality that can take place within and beyond the human expression as we know it. We are part of a Universal extent that is as yet, largely undiscovered. A tremendous potential lies within. The Universal awaits the return of its human children. Are humans mature enough to grasp the opportunity that individual living offers or must they continue to be unruly children, determined to stay in the playground of timeful experience because of the attractions that abound in their social surrounds?

Or will they heed the silent call of the spirit, turn their faces homeward bound, move with joyous hearts and eager minds and keep on going until they stand tall — spiritually tall — in final possession of all that matters in living?

May the choices be right.

About the author

JOSEPH RAFFA WAS born in 1927 in Fremantle, Western Australia. He enjoyed an idyllic childhood roaming the bush and the seashore. In his teens Joseph became a dedicated atheist, looking to science for answers to the riddles of life and the universe. Then, in his early twenties, he experienced a moment of discovery that transformed his life. As Joseph's life opened out spiritually following this awakening, he was inspired to put pen to paper to encourage others to embark on their own journey of discovery.

Joseph died of cancer in 2010, leaving behind a legacy of inspirational writing which is now being made available to a wider audience. Visit www.towardsthesilentheart.com for more information about Joseph and his books.

Other books by Joseph Raffa

Beside Still Waters

ISBN 9780987227676

This beautiful collection of essays touches on the universal search for meaning and inspires readers to reach out for the still waters of the spirit.

The human heart longs for peace and harmony. It seeks a restful haven from the relentless busyness of everyday life, drawing us to spend tranquil moments in natural surrounds that offer a brief respite from the hustle and bustle. There is a state of inner stillness, when the endless chatter of the mind has ceased, that a deeper understanding arises. These are the 'still waters' that bring new life to mankind, that lay claim to the heart and redirect the mind. These are the waters of peace, love and true togetherness that lift us up to divine heights of being and living.

The Silent Guardian

ISBN 9780987227669

A timely reminder of our spiritual journey and true purpose on Earth.

Joseph shares an inspirational message for those who care to listen.

Explore the planets, the outer reaches of space, the depths of the seas. Burrow into the earth, climb every mountain. When you have seen it all, you will still be left with the mystery of yourself. Turn and face this. Explore this. When you've travelled the extent and depth of the human expression, much of what you learn will be beyond the mind's capacity to convey through verbalisation. When heart speaks to heart, what more is there to say?

The Silent Guardian

Beyond the Cross

The Christ Collection

ISBN 9780987227652

A moving collection of inspired pieces about Jesus.

Joseph Raffa was a dedicated atheist when he set out in search of answers to the riddles of life and the universe. Then, in a blissful moment of discovery, the God the Bible speaks of, the Allah of Mohammed and the longed for Nirvana of the Buddhists came into his life. As his life opened out spiritually, Joseph began to have a deeper appreciation of Jesus, His life and His role in the spiritual awakening of Mankind. Visions and insights arose unbidden, in such a manner that their authenticity could not be questioned. The young man who was an atheist for a time, who cared not to read the Bible or take much notice of Christ and His life, found himself anchored in God and also writing pieces extolling the virtues, the wisdom and the love expressed by that super spiritual being of long ago.

Thank you for taking the time to read this book. Ratings and reviews are appreciated. If you enjoyed it, please Tweet/Share on your social media networks.